Henry Mayers Hyndman

A Summary of the Principles of Socialism

Written for the Democratic Federation

Henry Mayers Hyndman

A Summary of the Principles of Socialism
Written for the Democratic Federation

ISBN/EAN: 9783337312916

Printed in Europe, USA, Canada, Australia, Japan

Cover: Foto ©Suzi / pixelio.de

More available books at **www.hansebooks.com**

A

SUMMARY

OF THE

PRINCIPLES OF SOCIALISM

Written for the Democratic Federation.

BY

H. M. HYNDMAN AND WILLIAM MORRIS.

WILLIAM REEVES, 185, FLEET STREET, LONDON, E.C.

A SUMMARY

OF THE

PRINCIPLES OF SOCIALISM.

SOCIALISM, as a social and political system, depends altogether upon the history of mankind for a record of its growth in the past, and bases its future upon a knowledge of that history in so far as it can be accurately traced up to the present time. The groundwork of the whole theory is, that from the earliest period of their existence human beings have been guided by the power they possessed over the forces of nature to supply the wants arising as individual members of any society.

Thus Socialism rests upon political economy in its widest sense—that is, upon the manner in which wealth is produced and distributed by those who form part of society at a given time. Slavery, for instance, arose when men had reached such a point in the progress of the race that each labourer could produce by his work for a day, a week, a month, or a year more than was needed to keep him in health during that period. Then captives in war, instead of being killed, were enslaved, and the fruits of their labour, over and above their necesssary food, were taken by the conquering tribe; for though slavery arose in the nomadic state the earliest form of co-operation and ownership was of a tribe; and in the tribal relations common property was the rule alike in the soil and in the produce of labour.

As this common property broke up owing to the progress of the economical forms, the growth of exchange, the superiority of individuals or families in war or in the chase, classes or castes were gradually formed, resting in the first instance upon a necessary division of labour, though often existing, as in village communities, where a modified form of common property was still the rule. Thence, again, institutions developed through custom and law; religion sanctifying what had previously been found to be on the whole necessary or expedient. These institutions, though arising from the material power of man over nature, had in turn a great influence upon the manner in which that power was used, and appeared as the conservative side of human development conflicting with the progressive or revolutionary side, which necessarily follows upon the improvement and adaptation of the methods of producing food and wealth. From this essential and constant antagonism arises the conflict between classes in every civilisation of which we have any knowledge; and upon the struggles due to this conflict all progress has hitherto depended.

A slight consideration will serve to show that this is the true explanation of the growth of mankind. The first object of every animal, man included, is to feed itself and its offspring; and man began in the nomadic state by feeding upon fruits and berries. That the growth from the early brutish habits upwards to the taming of beasts and ordered agriculture was the process, not of thousands but of millions of years, is now admitted by all scientific writers on the records of primeval man. But the need for food was followed by the need for clothing, for warmth, for shelter; and each of these wants corresponded in turn with changing forms of social life as they were gratified. The whole, in fact, moved in one piece as the economical forms developed: the nomadic life of the woods and plains; the common property of the tribe or clan scanty and insufficient; the more confined area of operations as agriculture became an increasing business; the struggle with neighbouring tribes about rights of pasture or to obtain coveted spoils; the earlier or later introduction of slavery in place of wholesale slaughter of captives; the development of division of labour and exchange slowly breaking up the common property; the institution of private property in land, rendered necessary by the simultaneous improvements in agriculture; the increase of individual wealth, as cultivation and division of labour progressed on a larger scale, due to money-usury and slave-ownership; the construction of classes representing divergent interests; the struggle between the various classes and those above them; the enormous development of the slave class and the poorer citizens in Greece and still more in Rome; the gradual formation of customs, laws, religions growing out of these ever-changing, ever-progressing, economical forms; the constant appeals of the privileged orders to these customs, laws, and religious doctrines as the wisdom of the past not to be rudely shaken by the new-fangled, subversive theories of revolutionists, who were themselves but the unconscious exponents of such inevitable modifications — a careful study of each link in the chain of this long development, will show clearly how man in society has been the result of ages on ages of slow growth, in which the individual is lost in utter insignificance, and special inventions such as fire, the wheel, the mining, smelting, and working of metals, become manifestly but the inevitable results of the social state which produces them.

Leaving on one side the civilisations of Egypt and Eastern Asia, important as they are to a knowledge of our social growth—for only seventy generations of thirty years each take us back to a period when Britain was practically unknown, and Roman civilisation was in its infancy—it is sufficient to deal briefly with the decay of the Roman Empire, the feudal institutions which sprang up on its overthrow, and, more in detail, with the special circumstances which have influenced the progress of the people of Western Europe to the existing capitalist rule. The fact that the ancient civilisations of Greece and Rome were supported by open and acknowledged slavery of the mass of the producing class, renders all comparison of democracy, in the modern sense, with the so-called democracies of Greek or Roman society utterly futile. The economical and social conditions are entirely different.

Those Greek republics, which have so often been the theme for adulation on the part of democratic orators, poets, and artists, were themselves but close oligarchies; and the slave-class below was the basis of the whole super-structure alike at Athens, Corinth, and Sparta. The very numbers of the slaves show how completely the social arrangement was accepted as inevitable; for at Athens there were at least 120,000 slaves to 20,000 citizens, while at Corinth the slaves at one period numbered 460,000. Moreover, economical causes having produced slavery, force was long little needed to maintain the supremacy of the upper classes, who could carry on their own warfare among themselves almost undisturbed by fears of a slave revolt. In Rome the same forms appeared in rather different clothing, though in both the slaves were often learned, highly-trained men, widely different from the ignorant human machines whom we are accustomed to associate in our minds with the word slaves. In Rome, the insurrections of the slaves were more numerous and more formidable than in Greece. But, in this case, too, the conflicts between the various sections of the privileged classes were almost undisturbed, if we except the great insurrection of Spartacus, by the efforts at enfranchisement on the part of the slaves, who rarely timed their risings well and were massacred wholesale in Italy and Sicily at comparatively little cost of life to their masters.

Early in the record the slave-industry, controlled by the powerful landlord-capitalists of Rome and the other great cities of the Empire, began to crush out and even to enslave the small freeholders who had arisen on the break up of the tribes, or who belonged to conquered nations. Their independent work, with a few slaves around them, could make no head against the enormous production for gain which their large competitors carried on. The Licinian Law, and the agitations of the Gracchi were meant to protect the vigorous yeomen from forcible and still more from economical expropriation. But the movement was too strong to be resisted. Large properties grew steadily larger, and these great farms ruined not only Italy but other portions of the empire. The soil, though rich, was exhausted in the course of generations by ceaseless over-cropping for profit alone; the slave class of the country supported a useless and very numerous slave class in the towns; and the condition of the poor, free, Roman citizen became so bad that economically it could scarcely be worse. Thus, the prosperity of the whole empire was steadily sapped, and some regions have scarcely recovered the process unto this day. The Eastern Provinces, which had a history of their own even throughout the period of Roman domination, suffered less than the rest, whilst they provided the great proprietors of the metropolis with their luxuries, and thus regained in part by commerce what they lost by tribute.

The whole system of production and exchange was such that mercenary armies were needed to replace the old independent military service. Rome followed in the path of Carthage. Slowly the economical forms changed, and afterwards the social and political. From what seemed to contemporary observers the most dangerous or most worthless portions of the existing civilisation, a new life arose and progress followed. Out of the rottenness of the Roman Empire of the West, the slaves within and the barbarians from without formed the nucleus of another society. The spread of a new revolutionary Asiatic creed, with a higher morality than the popular forms of Paganism, was accompanied throughout the empire by a rising spirit among the slave class which provided its earliest converts, and the barbarian invaders, driven onwards probably by the exhaustion of their own sources of food supply found that the inhabitants of the territories they overran almost welcomed them. The downfall of the Roman Empire of the West was, in short, due to the necessary growth of fresh forces below, which took the place of worn-out forms that hampered the advance.

Thenceforward slavery in its old form faded into modern serfdom; and Catholicism, true to its origin, strove to uproot both, whilst maintaining an equality of conditions at the start within its own body. Organised Christianity exercised, in some sense, as a religion, the power which had belonged to Rome as a centre of empire. In Western Europe, through the long period of the so-called dark ages—so hard to understand even by the full light of modern scientific research—new methods of production and exchange were taking the place of the old, new relations were being established between men as individuals, and men as classes. The decay of the Roman roads shut off the new communities to a great extent from one another, as the disbandment of the legions loosened the bonds of authority; a new art and a new literature grew up in each country, founded doubtless on the old, but fresh and vigorous indeed compared with the bastard work of servile copyists, which well reflected the degradation of Greek as well as of Roman civilisation; new laws and new customs necessarily grew out of the changed conditions, notwithstanding the partial influence of the Roman codes. Above all there was the new religion, which, rising triumphant over the old pagan creeds, had nevertheless adopted, perforce, the old pagan ceremonial and the old pagan festivities; in the same way that the serfs and domestic retainers, though holding far different relations to their superiors from those of the slaves to their masters, still used the agricultural implements and handled almost the same primitive machines as the slave class, who were, so to say, their economical ancestors.

Instead of the combined landlord and capitalist controlling tens, hundreds, or thousands of toilers on his estate through a bailiff, we have the disruption again of village communities of free men—traces of which can be found in all European countries to this day—developing into a system of serfdom where the serfs were bound to the soil, but bound also by direct personal relations to their masters. So, too, as these changes acted and reacted new class-struggles took the place of the old. Oppressors and oppressed, dominant and servile, lord and burgher, master and craftsman, seigneur and serf, stood in antagonism, as mankind were feeling their way to a wider economical development. Centuries of disintegration and reconstruction were needed to bring forth the complete feudal system; and the earliest development of modern trade and commerce took place on the shores of that great inland sea which for ages was the cradle of western civilisation. Venice, Genoa, Pisa, followed in the footsteps of Tyre, Corinth, and Carthage. Rome, instead of being the metropolis of a great empire, became the head-quarters of a religious organisation which exercised an influence that reached the uttermost parts of the western world.

That the influence of the Catholic Church was, in the main, used in the interest of the people against the dominant classes can scarcely now be disputed; nor that the equality of conditions to start with in the organisation itself was one of the great causes of its extraordinary success throughout the so-called dark ages. Catholicism, in its best period, raised one continuous protest against serfdom and usury, as early Christianity, in its best form, had denounced slavery and usury too. But the economical tendencies were too strong for any protest to be much regarded at first. Divison of labour, and the structure of society thence resulting, at a time when the powers of man over nature were still limited, gave power and importance to the warrior caste and the priestly caste over the mere hinds and handicraftsmen. Yet, even in the earliest period of feudalism, the risings of the trading class, and with them at times the peasants and artizans, against the nobles and territorial clergy, were neither few nor far between. The engagement of the knight and his retainers to defend the agriculturists, handicraftsmen, and traders who clustered round the fortress of which he was the lord, led to demands on his side which the burghers and their people resented. In Italy, in Germany, in France, and in England, the great nobles and their feudatories were in time confronted by municipalities with privileges granted in return for services rendered, and the great cities of Flanders and Western Germany almost rivalled the Italian Republics in the influence they manifested of town over country which then first began to be felt in its modern form. The definite struggle between the nobility and the bourgeoisie, therefore, took shape at the same time, though assuming different aspects, in different countries.

On, the other hand, the unorganised risings of the peasantry, such as the Peasants' War in England, the great insurrections of the Jacquerie in France, and of the serfs in Germany, were the attempts of the proletariat of the middle-ages to obtain some improvement in their lot apart from the traders, whose position was of course very different. The serf of the middle-ages shows but as a sorry figure, indeed, in all countries, as compared with that splendid chivalry, whose resplendent armour and noble individual prowess have been the theme of so much glorification. Yet, for centuries, these despised churls provided in the form of food and wares, furnished by the number of days' work due to their lord for nothing, the means of providing all the magnificence which decked out the baron, the abbot, and the fair ladies of the court. Everywhere, however, at the height of the feudal domination, the handicraftsman, more especially at the later period which preceded its disruption, was a free man. The contrast between the position of such a man or the yeoman, and the villeins, was most striking in every respect. The latter were mere chattels: the former were independent men; more independent perhaps in England than the people as a body have ever been economically, socially, and politically, at any other period of our history.

For in England—and this it is which renders our own country the most fitting field for the study of modern development — the enfranchisement of the peasantry and their settlement upon the land as free yeomen, took place at a much earlier date than in any other nation. These yeomen were in fact the mainstay of England for several hundred years, and their influence can be traced in our national history before the enfranchisement of the serfs as a body.

great risings, however, of the fourteenth century, secured for the mass of our people that freedom and well-being which made common Englishmen for at least two centuries the envy of Europe. Serfdom was almost entirely done away, men were masters of themselves, their land, and their labour. Labourers and craftsmen were alike well-paid, well-fed people, who were not only in possession of the land which they might occupy and till, but were also entitled to rights of pasturage over large tracts of common land, since robbed from their descendants by the meanness of an usurping class who made laws in their own favour to sanctify pillage.

England, far more densely peopled at that time than is generally supposed, was in fact inhabited by perhaps the most vigorous, freedom-loving set of men the world ever saw, who, having shaken themselves free from the slavery of the feudal system, were still untrammelled by the worse slavery of commercialism and capital. The economical forms, the methods of production, were the direct cause of this universal well-being and sturdy independence. Instead of men working under the control of the landlord or the landlord-capitalist as slaves or serfs for the sake of wealth and profit for their owners, the yeomen were owners themselves of their own means of production, and produced for the use of the family, only paying a portion of such production as tithes, or dues, or taxes. Rent, in the sense of a competition price paid for the occupation of land, was at this period almost unknown in Northern and Western Europe as well as in these islands.

Production therefore being carried on for use, though

only in primitive fashion with small implements adapted to individual handling, most of the products being consumed or worked up into rude manufactures on the farm itself, only the superfluity after the yeoman and his family were well-fed and well-clothed came into exchange. And this exchange itself, like the production, was carried on by the individual. Craftsmen were economically as independent as the yeomen and free-labourers, though laws were early made (happily for many generations without effect) to limit their powers of combination, and to keep down the rates of wages which either they or the agricultural labourers could command. They also were in control of their means of production, and what they made was the result of their own labour on raw materials, which they in turn exchanged for other goods made by men as free as themselves, or were paid for by the lord or the abbot. Still the relations were in the main personal, and not pecuniary, still a man who earned wages for a day was by no means forced to compete with his neighbour for hire by an employer as a wage-earner all his life through.

The trade guilds which in the first instance were thoroughly democratic in their constitution, protected the craftsmen against unregulated competition, or from the attempt to oppress them in any way. Moreover, as it was easy then for a labourer to obtain a patch of land, and to remove himself wholly or in part from the wage-earners, so a journeyman apprentice starting in life as a mere worker could and generally did attain to the dignity of a master craftsman in mature age. The amount of capital to be amassed ere a man could work for himself was so small that no serious barrier was placed between the journeyman and independence; besides, the arrangements of the guilds were such that wherever a craftsmen wandered he was received as a brother of his particular craft. Although also the rest of Europe was behind England in the settlement of the people on the soil, the craft-guilds were even more important in the Low Countries and part of Germany in the Middle Ages than in England. Thus it should appear that in the record of the feudal development the period reached in each country when the peasant was a free man working for himself upon the land, and the craftsman was likewise a free man master of his own means of production represents the time of greatest individual prosperity for the people.

England, where this independence was on the whole earliest developed, presented on this very account a marked contrast to France where the risings of the Jacquerie had not resulted so well for the people as our own peasant insurrections. In Germany and Italy the rural population was much behind the townspeople though in Spain, the early communal forms being there retained, the peasants were better off. The really important point is that, under such conditions of production as those described, where the means of production are at the disposal of the individual, who also controls the exchange of the superfluity, perfect economical freedom, as well as political freedom or freedom before the law, is possible and indeed cannot be avoided. Men then had something worth fighting for at home and abroad, and were quite ready to spend their own blood and their own money in fighting for a cause which they held to be their own. Vicarious sacrifice of the lives of mercenary troops and posterity's money was nowise to their minds; they took note that such methods of warfare were at once cowardly and mean.

The Church as a collective body supplemented the needs of this thoroughly individualist society. The services rendered by the monasteries, priories, and nunneries to the people in the shape of constant employment on their estates, of almsgiving, maintenance of hospitals, schools, inns, maintenance of roads, have been systematically depreciated by middle-class historians; but these semi-socialist bodies were of the highest value in the economy of the middle-ages, more especially in England, and the lands which they held were used and their revenues applied in such manner that during their most flourishing period the noblest institutions were kept up by their aid. Permanent pauperism was unknown, and vagrancy was charitably restrained so long as these institutions were in existence. The services rendered by them in the direction of art and letters it is needless to recount.

But at the risk of being compelled to repeat later what is urged here, it is well to consider at this point the effect which the full development of the individual man and his power over his own tools, materials, and the objects he worked upon, had upon art. The ordinary opinion seems to be that art is bred and sustained by the luxury resulting from the present state of society, with its monstrous contrasts of riches and poverty. A very brief survey will be enough to show the falsity of this notion. The slave-served society of the classical peoples intellectual and highly-refined but simple in life and free, in Greece at any rate, from what is now called luxury, looked upon art as a necessity, and found no serious obstacle in the way of surrounding the daily life of man with beauty. The rigid caste system of the feudal hierarchy kept up the most violent arbitrary distinctions between classes, but had no temptation to extend those distinctions to the minds and imaginations of men, and no means whereby it could do so. Thus the artificer was left free to express, according to his capacity, the ideas which he shared with the noble, developing as a class a hereditary skill and dexterity in the handling of the simple tools of the time.

Under the craft-gilds of the latter middle-ages the industrial arts were divided rigidly into corporations, but inside those corporations division of labour was yet in its infancy; so that each fully instructed craftsman was master of his own handicraft, and was by all surrounding circumstances encouraged to be an *artist* whose labour could not be wholly irksome to him. By this means the taste and knowledge of what art was then possible were spread widely among the people and became instinctive in them, so that all manufactured articles as it were grew beautiful in the unobtrusive and effortless way that the works of nature grow. The result of five centuries of this popular art is obvious in the outburst of splendid genius which lit up the days of the Italian Renaissance: the strange rapidity with which that splendour faded as commercialism advanced is proof enough that this great period of art was born not of dawning commercialism but of the freedom of the intelligence of labour from the crushing weight of the competition market, a freedom which it enjoyed throughout the middle-ages.

The exquisite armour of the knights, their swords and lances of perfect temper, the splendid and often humorous decorations of the stone and wood-work in the cathedrals, churches and abbeys, the illuminations of the missals, the paintings of the time, the manner in which beautiful designs and tracery nestled even in places where it might be thought that the human eye could rarely or never reach, nay, even such fragments of ordinary domestic furniture and utensils as have been preserved, all show that the art of the middle Ages, like the art of Greece, was something loved and cherished and made perfect for its own sake, that beauty welled up unbidden from the spontaneous flow of the ideas of the time. But just at this period of the fullest individual perfection the necessities of competition, arising out of economical changes in the conditions of labour which have yet to be traced, gradually turned the workman from the mediæval artist-craftsman into the mere artisan of the capitalist system, and almost entirely destroyed the attractiveness of his labour; so that when about the end of the 17th century the work-shop system of labour which had pushed out the gild system was struggling to perfect its speciality, the division of labour namely, wherein the unit of labour is not a single workman but a group, it found the romance, the soul, both of the higher and the decorative arts, gone though the commonplace or body of them still existed.

How then was the artist-craftsman thus turned into a mere artisan? How did the competition arise in such shape that not free rivalry in the creation of beauty but fierce antagonism in the greed for gain became the rule of production? Once more the economical forms changed and destruction of the old society was the inevitable result.

As the feudal system was introduced into different European countries at different periods, as again the gradual conversion of serfs into free yeomen and lifeholders was by no means simultaneous in every nation, as further the formation of the craft-gilds varied, so the decay and final disruption of the feudal system took place at widely separated periods of time. In England the end of the wars of the Roses saw the commencement of this rapid disintegration. During those wars the barons had largely increased the numbers of their retainers, and had thus impoverished themselves; the people as a whole standing aloof from the bootless and bloody Civil War between the houses of York and Lancaster. Many of the ancient nobility were utterly exterminated in the course of the struggle; and the successors to their estates, when peace was finally proclaimed on the accession of Henry VII., carried on a process, which had begun even earlier, of turning out their now useless retainers to shift for themselves. These people formed the first set of vagrants and wandering bands, who without house, home, land or any recognised position in, or claim upon society, roamed through the country in search of labour and food. The monasteries, however, were still in full organisation and provided to a large extent for these wanderers.

But at the same time pressure was brought to bear upon the innumerable small farmers and yeomen, common land was ruthlessly enclosed, and the nobles adopted every conceivable device to enrich themselves at the expense of those who had a better title to the land than they had. Hence more vagrants, more homeless and a manifest decay in the real strength of the kingdom. Here again the reasons of the change were economical. The nobles wanted money to pay the debts which they had incurred during the wars, and also to maintain themselves at Court which they now more regularly frequented; just at this time too the Flanders market afforded a most profitable outlet for wool. Hence it was advantageous for the landholders in every way to remove men and substitute sheep; since pasture farming needed fewer hands than arable and sheep paid better than human beings. This process of expropriation therefore went relentlessly on during the whole of the latter part of the sixteenth century in spite of numerous statutes against such action and the never-ceasing protests of men like More, Latimer, &c., against the mischief that was being done. Thus by degrees a landless class was being formed with no property beyond the bare force of labour in their bodies; and these people were slowly driven into the towns where they formed the germ of our modern city proletariat.

The breakdown of the feudal system led in almost every country to the establishment of a despotism, and England formed no exception to the rule. Henry VIII. and Thomas Cromwell answer closely enough to Louis XIII. and Richelieu. It was the object of king and minister alike that the crown should be supreme, and to a large extent they succeeded in attaining it: though Cromwell, less dexterous than the

French minister, lost his own head after having removed the heads of so many others. But the Reformation and the consequent downfal of the monasteries were the most important events in English history between the Peasant's War and the great industrial revolution at the end of the eighteenth century. The Reformation in Germany was as far from being a movement of the people as it was in England; in France also the Protestants were as little representative of peasantry as the Catholic nobles. Luther himself, that fierce champion of individualism, was a bitter opponent of the peasants in their risings against the nobles. In fact the Reformation everywhere, though partly directed against undoubted abuses in the church, was a thorough middle-class movement representing fully middle-class aspirations for individual aggrandisement here and hereafter.

In England the king was shrewd enough to put himself at its head knowing that more solid gain was to be had by the plunder of the church than by maintaining a resolute attitude as Defender of a Faith that gave him nothing and took much. Thus the monasteries were destroyed, and the king was enabled to reconcile the barons to this pillage by giving them a good share of the plunder of the lands of the church and the people. Nearly one-half of the land of England, which had up to this time been used to a large extent for public purposes, now became the property of a number of nobles and courtiers who recognised little or no duty of trusteeship, and who even allowed the public roads which the monks had kept up to go to ruin, as they suffered the magnificent abbeys to decay or be turned into quarries for building materials. Henceforth the people of England had no hold upon their own land; and all the duties which the monks and nuns had filled in the economy of the middle-ages fell into abeyance and were left unperformed. As to the inhabitants of the monasteries, the monks and nuns, friars and sisters who were turned out of their houses, they joined the army of miserable vagrants now yearly increasing on the public highways. With no means of earning a livelihood, they and the discharged retainers, the expropriated yeomen and the discharged hinds, were a never-ceasing source of annoyance to the classes which had driven them out to starve; whilst the very abolition of the monasteries, which intensified the mischief, deprived these poor people of their last hope of succour.

Such was the pressure on the peasantry, owing to the enclosures, the robberies of commons, and the seizure of the Church Lands, that in spite of the infamous atrocities wreaked upon all disturbers of order and upon the wretched vagrants themselves, who were hanged and disembowelled, tortured and flogged in batches, there were a whole series of insurrections after the suppression of the monasteries, some of which were supported by the well-to-do, and even, as in the case of the insurrection of the Northern Earls, by the nobles themselves. The new system of production for profit and constant competition for wages, involving though it did progress, in the sense of producing more wealth with fewer hands, by the division of labour and co-operation, was thus not introduced without a frightful and bloody class struggle on the part of the people to maintain their old individual independence. The risings were put down with frightful cruelty, however, and the laws against vagrants who were forced to wander by the changed conditions of agriculture, were harsher than ever under the reign of Queen Elizabeth, the monarch whose reign is supposed to embrace the most glorious period of English history.

It is worthy of remark also that during the whole of the sixteenth century the attempts made to stop the uprooting of the people from the soil by law were absolutely unavailing. The class now gaining power in the country, namely the landlords with bailiffs, and the large farmers, who both regarded the land only as a means of making gain, rode roughshod over the enactments of Parliament in favour of the poor; though they took care to give full force to all those which tended in any way to strengthen their own power. The same with the rising bourgeoisie, who rapidly gained influence under Elizabeth, and used it as far as possible to remove those restrictions upon usury, and laws in favour of the labourers, which in the middle-age polity had balanced the futile statutes against combination. By the end of the sixteenth century consequently all was ready in our country for the gradual formation of a competitive wage-slave class divorced from the soil and deprived of the means of production, which class must therefore be in a growing degree at the mercy of the classes that possessed the land and the capital.

The increasing amount of capital also needed for success in business as the markets grew, and the town supplied not only the country but foreign lands, gradually broke down the democratic constitution of the trade-gilds. It was no longer a matter of course for a capable apprentice and journeyman to become in due time master of the craft. On the contrary, the minority, the capitalist masters, exercised increasing authority within the gild and turned its machinery to the disadvantage of the poorer members. Thus, between the landless proletariat, which was being created by social and economical oppression, and the landlords letting land for money-rentals in place of the old feudal services due to the nobles, the middle or capitalist class, the bourgeoisie, was growing up, whose bitter antagonism to the landlords has been carried on, as the necessary result of economical progress, even to our own day. Farmers who farmed for profit, and merchants and manufacturers who employed their men to gain a profit from their competitive labour, quite replaced the simpler economy of the middle ages, when nearly all were farming or producing for direct use.

During this period of fearful suffering for the mass of the people, when the foundations of our modern capitalist society were laid, the greatest and most sudden development of commerce ever seen on the planet took place, and international production and exchange gradually overshadowed the old national markets and methods of working up home products. The discovery of America and of the new route round the Cape to India and China, the conquest of Mexico and Peru, the conquest of Asia Minor by the Ottoman Turks, all took place within two generations. A new world of adventure, a new world of thought, were opened up before mankind. A flood of the precious metals was poured into Europe from America giving in many ways increased power to the trading and profit-making class, and increasing the accumulation of capital. The spoils of Mexico and Peru, the wealth of all kinds gained by commerce, forced on the development at headlong speed. Spain was ruined by the very circumstances which gave her strength. The Italian cities lost their commercial supremacy from this time forward, owing in part to the decay of Asia Minor and the breakdown of the overland connection with the East, following upon the Turkish rule, and partly to the change in the relative importance of the trade to America and the West Indies. In consequence England, France, Spain, Portugal, and the Low Countries became the chief competitors for the commerce of the world, Venice lending her spare capital to the Dutch at good rates of interest, thus encouraging the very competition that must eventually ruin her. Hence arose the commercial wars and commercial rivalries of the seventeenth and eighteenth centuries, in which Spain at the first had every apparent advantage.

Meanwhile in England feudalism had been completely destroyed as a system, and commercialism was being substituted. Keeping pace with the change in the forms of production, progress in all directions helped on the new development. The spread of printing destroyed the monopoly of letters which had been enjoyed by the clergy and the learned of high rank; the application of gunpowder to war rendered the common man-at-arms the superior of the most gorgeously equipped knight. Thus the increase of general knowledge sapped superstition, and the musket swept away the last relics of warrior chivalry.

As the markets expanded also, the results of these great changes in every direction became more and more apparent. The miserable state of the internal communications forced Englishmen more and more into foreign commerce, which was rendered exceptionally profitable, not only by the discovery of new markets that gave great returns to the trader, but also by the useful adjuncts of piracy and slavery. To keep pace with this growth of commerce wider organisation of labour was needed, and, therefore, as already stated, the group of workmen toiling under the superintendence of the master, with a more and more regulated division of labour, supplanted the old handicraft. Workshops grew larger and larger, small factories were formed in certain trades. The workmen ceased to own any portion of their own product: that, as a whole, went into the hand of the employer who paid for a part of its value in wages; in the same way the agricultural labourer ceased to have any interest in the crops which he raised: they, too belonged to the farmer, subject to a deduction for rent to the landlord; and the labourer also received a part of the value of his labour in wages. Production had become or was rapidly becoming social: appropriation and exchange remained under the control of the individual.

During the whole of the seventeenth and the first half of the eighteenth century this process went on. Organised handicraft, factory industry, and house industry, were still to be seen together. A good many yeomen remained in some districts, but they were becoming continually less numerous; though the agricultural regions were still much more populous than the towns, and so remained until the end of the eighteenth century. On every side commerce was the one prevailing object, and to that all was subordinated. Religion naturally adapted itself to the tone of the time; and the Protestantism of England became what it has ever since remained—essentially a creed for the successful trafficker in wares or in souls.

All through Europe the system of to-day in credit, competition, and national rivalry was practically established, and the era of foreign conquest and colonial empire began. But still the conflict of the middle-class against the king and the landed aristocracy loomed ahead. Wise sovereigns had shown true policy in yielding to and even in fostering the growing power. Others, perhaps more upright but certainly less dexterous, precipitated the struggle. In England it first took shape in serious organised warfare. The bloody civil war of the seventeenth century was clearly a struggle between the ideas of divine right and landowner supremacy on the one side, against the sanctity of profit and freedom for the middle-class on the other. The economical victory already gained in the counting-house was but confirmed in the field; and the reign of Cromwell served as an introduction to the thorough middle-class rule of William III.

From this time forward the question was merely how long it would take for the middle-class to establish in outward seeming that supremacy which, in regard to production, they had already to a large extent secured. Their power was still somewhat hampered by the relics of the old middle-age restrictions even after the accession of William of Orange and the House of Brunswick had virtually proclaimed that capitalism, with its debt funded for payment by posterity, its standing mercenary army, and its worldwide international production and exchange, had become master of the economical, and, in the strict sense, social field. But division of labour was carried farther and farther, trade and commerce developed exceedingly, the settlements in America and the factories in India helped on the growth, until in the eighteenth century, the period had manifestly arrived for yet another development which would enable the productive forces to supply the ever-growing market.

Prior to this new manifestation of the powers of man over nature and of the method in which, under such social conditions as now existed, these powers were turned to the sole advantage of a class, the condition of the English worker was better than it had been at any period since the fifteenth century. His wages both in town and country bore a higher ratio to the cost of living than at any intermediate time. Agriculture had recovered in some degree from the depression of the sixteenth century, owing to the demand for cereals in the growing comercial cities; and the artisan, under the division of labour and the group system of factory production, was in a more favourable position than he had been when home competition was more severe and foreign markets were less open.

In France, on the contrary, the peasantry had not gained ground against the barons to nearly the same extent, nor were the bourgeoisie nearly so advanced in their political struggle as the corresponding classes in England. Though the serfs had to some degree been settled upon the land, the oppression of the nobles and the pressure of taxation, owing to the wars of Louis XIV., ground down the poor to a level wholly unknown on this side of the Channel. Moreover, the rush of speculation and commercialism produced a far more rapid and complete deterioration of the character of the whole upper classes in Paris, and in France generally, than it did in London and England.

Thus at the end of the eighteenth century France was fully prepared for a political and social, England was more ready for an industrial, revolution. The ideas of the time were much the same in both countries; but whereas our middle-class had taken order with their king and his aristocrats in the seventeenth century, and capital had secured its firm foothold at that time alike in town and country, France had yet to pass through a whole series of events parallel to what had already taken place here generations before. The English Revolution, the American War of Independence, stirring the minds of the middle-class and the people, the utter degradation of the French nobility by the scenes in the Rue Quincampoix occasioned by their endeavour to make gain out of Law's Mississippi scheme and similar ventures, the destruction of faith in the prevailing religion among the educated by Voltaire and Rousseau, and the Encyclopædists, the prevailing misery among the entire population, which was totally disregarded by the nobles and the court, were factors that all tended relentlessly to a political overthrow.

The change in the conditions of the time had not

been recognised. Those economical and social displacements which had already prepared the revolution in the body of society had passed unheeded; and thus the French Revolution, which was clearly predicted by a few careful observers, came upon the world at large as a surprise. It was a rising against a tyranny alike corrupt, mean, and obsolete. Its influence spread rapidly at first and, coming after the noble American Declaration of Independence, produced a great effect in every European country, not least in England. That glorious struggle for Liberty, Equality, and Fraternity, which began in 1789, that temporary alliance of the bourgeoisie and the proletariat, though it gave rise to some splendid episodes for the people, ended in victory for the bourgeoisie alone. The really great names of the French revolution have, of course, been honoured by middle-class abuse. Napoleon, the hero of reaction, used the enthusiasm born of revolution to spread his self-seeking imperialism through Europe, and enabled reactionists in other countries to pose as the champions of national freedom.

The effect of the great revolutionary war upon England, and the increased power which the long conflict placed in the hands of the aristocratic and capitalist classes, was most disastrous from every point of view. Political progress was thrown back nearly a century, social reforms were indefinitely postponed, and the new industrial forces went almost without heed or protest into the hands of the profit-making class. And these industrial forces were of a magnitude, and produced effects the like of which had never been seen in the world before. As the great geographical and mercantile discoveries at the end of the sixteenth century, with the rapid development of shipping, ended by giving England the control of commerce; so the great inventions at the end of the eighteenth century resulted in giving this country the lead in industry. But the effect upon the people was terrible almost from the beginning. At first a few benefited by the increased powers of production alike in labouring on the land and with respect to working up raw materials; and the initial steps were taken towards the formation of an aristocracy of labour to protect, by means of secret societies, the interests of the skilled artisans. But the power of machinery soon broke down these earlier combinations. The cottage industry was ere long completely destroyed. In every branch of trade the development became so extraordinary that nothing but a constant supply of fresh hands to work the machines, and in turn an improvement of machines to restrain the demands of the hands could keep pace with the growing markets opened by the increasing cheapness of production.

Competition took another great stride in advance. Poor Irishmen, driven from their own country by landlord rascality and oppression, came in to compete at the lowest standard of life with the already impoverished Englishmen. Towns grew in magnitude with amazing rapidity as steam and greater knowledge of the use of water power increased the size of the factories and the number of men, women, and children who could work under the control of one employer. From being an agricultural country England in the course of fifty or sixty years became essentially a country of great cities with a proletariat under the control of the capitalist class in a worse condition (this all official reports show) than any slave class of ancient times had ever lived in. For ere long the capitalist class, now almost at the height of its economical power, had swept away entirely the restrictions imposed by the middle-age polity. Freedom of contract between the pauper and the plutocrat, unrestrained competition between men and women in order that they might be able to get enough out of the product of their labour merely to keep body and soul together, wholesale slaughter of children by overwork and insufficient nourishment in unhealthy, overheated factories and ill-ventilated mines—the whole system was based upon never-ending oppression of the most horrible kind. Wages fell in proportion to the cost of living at the very time when enormous fortunes were being accumulated in the cotton, wool, silk, iron, and other industries. Women and children were brought in to reduce the wages of their own fathers and brothers by competing for under-pay.

The legislature, under the direct control of the classes interested in maintaining this atrocious slavery under the guise of freedom, refused at first even to bring in laws to prevent babes from three to nine years of age from being worked fourteen, fifteen, sixteen hours a day. Capital had full swing in every direction and ground down the body of the people into a hopeless degradation from which they have never yet emerged. Risings there were from time to time in the earlier part of this century against this fearful oppression brought about by sheer greed for gain. But they were all unsuccessful, and not until the half of the century had passed away were any effective laws enacted, at the instance of such men as Robert Owen, to check the capitalist class in their furious haste to be rich at the expense of the men, women, and children, whom they robbed wholesale of their labour and ruined in their health. For now man was slave to the machine, no longer a free agent in any sense. Division of labour in the workshop faded into the great factory industry; and machines, as they were introduced, served not to benefit the community and lessen the amount of labour needed to produce wealth but absolutely to increase the hours of labour, to degrade the workers more and more, and, by frequently throwing hands out into street, gradually to form a fringe of labour, ever on the verge of pauperism—ready to take the lowest wages, even when an impetus to trade rendered the capitalist class anxious for more hands. This introduction of machinery, this complete domination of the capitalist class and sweeping expropriation of the labour of the workers, piled up the wealth for the few which enabled us to come out triumphant from the great war.

But whence came the wealth thus accumulated by the few out of the labour of others—by the capitalist farmers in the country, by the capitalist factory owners and loiterers in the towns? Out of the excessive labour of the workers who were hopelessly divorced from the means of production, and were compelled to sell their labour-force to the capitalist for the lowest subsistence wages. The economical law of such competition among the workers as that which has gone on in England since the end of the eighteenth century, is admitted by the capitalists, and their fuglemen, the political economists, themselves. The one object of production being production for profit, the capitalist of course buys the labour-force which the needy worker is driven to sell at the lowest possible price in wages. This price, it is now agreed, corresponds on the average to the social needs represented by the standard of life in the class to which the seller of the labour-force belongs. At times the wages may, and do, fall far below this level of necessary subsistence, at other times combination among the workers, or a period of exceptionally prosperous trade, may temporarily raise them above this level. But the tendency is always as stated; nor does the existence of an aristocracy of labour modify the truth of the proposition. But when the capitalist, whether a farmer or a factory-lord, has bought the destitute worker's labour-force on the market, he does so with the intention of applying it to the growing of his crops, or to the manufacture of the raw materials which he has purchased at their market value. Labour-force embodied in commodities, the cost of production or re-production, that is, of articles reckoned useful in the social conditions of the time, is the basis and measure of their average exchange-value when brought forward for exchange. In the first two or three hours of the day's work, however, the labouring class whose labour-force is thus purchased, refund to the employing class the full value of the wages which they receive in return for the whole day's work. But the entire product of the day's work, or the week's work, or the month's work, or the year's work, is at the control of the capitalist who thus appropriates two-thirds or three quarters of the labourers' work without paying for it.

In the factory, that is to say, and to an ever increasing degree on the farm, the labourers work as a portion of an association; their labour is socialised in the highest degree. But both their products and the exchange of their products are at the disposal of individuals who compete with one another for gain above, as the workers compete against one another for bare subsistence below.

Here then are the two main features of our modern system of production for profit. *First.* The labourers on the average replace the value of their wages for the capitalist class in the first few hours of their day's work; the exchange value of the goods produced in the remaining hours of the day's work constitutes so much embodied labour which is unpaid; and this unpaid labour so embodied in articles of utility, the capitalist class, the factory owners, the farmers, the bankers, the brokers, the shopkeepers, and their hangers-on the landlords, divide among themselves in the shape of profits, interests, discounts, commissions, rent, &c. *Second.* The other feature is the antagonism between the socialised method of production and the individualised system of exchange. This brings about unmitigated anarchy in the shape of a world-wide crisis every ten years, which throws labourers out of work when they are as anxious to toil for subsistence as ever they were; and piles up quantities of goods which these very labourers are eager to buy, but which owing to the crisis they cannot earn the means of purchasing, because the capitalist class will not employ them unless a profit is to be made, and this profit is rendered impossible by the very glut of the goods. Such crises have now occurred every ten years since 1825, and owing to these, men and women have been continually thrown out of work and flung into misery from no fault whatever of their own.

The introduction of fresh machines is similarly against workers, tending as it does to increased uncertainty of employment and to reduce skilled workers to a lower class. Thus the tendency is to produce not merely a destitute proletariat forced to remain as a class wage-slaves to their masters, body-slaves to the machine, their life long; but also a fringe of labour employed at scant wages in "good times," thrown into pauperism and starvation in bad. Hence freedom of contract between those who have no means of production, and those who have a monopoly of them, simply involves the most terrible economical tyranny the world has yet seen: the surplus value provided under this illusory freedom out of unpaid labour enables the idle classes and their dependants to live in luxury at the expense of persistent overwork and misery for the producers themselves.

Thus individual exchange uncontrolled by thought of collective advantage brings about fearful anarchy in every direction, which is a satire indeed upon the middle-class cuckoo cry of "order, order."

Children are ill-nurtured and underfed, women are worked to within a few hours of pregnancy, the conditions of existence for the mass of the people are such that health, happiness, and morality are impossible, and still the capitalist class and their champions, the political economists, tell us that such is the inevitable outcome of our mock civilisation. Nor is there any real standard of honour among the competitors for wealth themselves.

Having robbed the labourers wholesale of their labour, they proceed to rob one another by underselling, adulteration and fraud. As a general result of the system mere pecuniary relations are paramount. How to make money is the be-all and end-all of this ruinous system of competitive production for profit. Love, honour, ability, beauty, all are in the market—going, going, going, gone! knocked down to the highest bidder.

Art! that necessarily fades under such conditions; and machine-work, literally and figuratively, is the product of the time. This has been gradually brought about through the operation of the economical forms whose development has been briefly traced. Throughout the 18th century the idea that the making of goods is the end and aim of manufacture still struggled, with ever-increasing feebleness, against the real view of capitalism, that manufacture has no essential aim save profit for the capitalist-class, and mere occupation for the workman: occupation, that is, daily leisureless labour with no pretence to attractiveness in it, rewarded by a livelihood whose standard is forced down by competition to the lowest point which will be endured without active discontent.

This view is accepted as a matter past discussion by the fully-developed capitalism of the 19th century which has in its turn supplanted the workshop, with its groups of workmen each skilled in a narrow round of labour, by the factory with its machines tended by women and children or by a mere labourer of whom neither skill nor intelligence is necessarily required. This system with its unavoidable consequence that the greater and (commercially) more important part of the wares it produces are made for the consumption of poor and degraded people without leisure or taste wherewith to discern beauty, without money or labour to pay for excellence of workmanship—this system makes labour so repulsive and burdensome that art, in the long run, is impossible under it. Instead of the pleasant, intellectual, fruitful labour of the middle-ages, we have the barren, hideous drudgery of the factory and the cotton-mill. While it lasts all the ordinary surroundings of life must of necessity be ugly and brutal, and what of art is left for a time, depending as it does, not on its own life, but on the memory of past days of glory and beauty, must be produced by men of exceptional gifts, living isolated amidst the ugliness and brutality of their own time and protesting against the spirit of their own age. Thus the capitalist system threatens to dry up the very springs of all art, that is, of the external beauty of life, and to reduce the world to a state of barbarism.

The proletariat, however, as already remarked, were not crushed into this helplessness in England without having struggled against the meanest tyranny that ever oppressed them. From the end of the last century, when Trade Societies were established throughout the kingdom, vainly endeavouring to make head against the steadily growing power of capital, the working classes kept up an increasing agitation in favour of a more reasonable lot for themselves and their children. Another serious class fight had begun. What the workers saw was this:—that the introduction of machinery, though it might give wealth to the capitalist class and to the country at large, brought with it for them starvation and intolerable misery, owing to the displacement of the old methods and the competition of the labour of women and children with that of grown men.

During the first three-quarters of the eighteenth century also the people, as we have seen, were on the whole better off, their wages would buy them more and better food and raiment than for two centuries before. Consequently the pressure being sudden was more severely felt and more vigorously resisted than it is to-day. The workers saw that the unregulated introduction of machines meant for them ruin; as Sir James Steuart, the famous economist, plainly stated it must, ten years before the publication of "The Wealth of Nations." They, therefore, in the first place attacked the machines themselves; and bands of workpeople under the name of Luddites destroyed machinery in many industrial centres, with the impression that thus they were striking heavy blows at the real enemy. As a matter of course their adversaries were not the inert machines, which only produced more wealth at the cost of less and less expenditure of human labour, but the class appropriation of these improvements which gave to the labourers, owing to competition among themselves for employment, a less and less proportionate share of the wealth created.

For the cheapening of the products did not benefit the workers as a class. It only enabled them to take a lower average wage in times of pressure without absolute starvation; whilst the uncertainty arising from constant improvements and the competition of their own families rendered their position even worse than the mere amount of wages for long hours and excessive overwork would betoken. Thus the very circumstances which should have bettered their condition and rendered their life more easy, actually pressed them down to a lower standard of existence.

Not until 1802 was any step taken to recognise even that children were overworked, and the Act then passed was wholly abortive. In 1814 the capitalist class even succeeded in removing the last vestige of the old restrictions notwithstanding the overwhelming array of petitions from the workers against any such action. At this time it must be remembered that all combinations among the workers to raise wages, or to strike for any reason whatsoever, were illegal. Soon afterwards the great war came to an end which had so much strengthened the power of the landowners, farmers and capitalists, at the expense of the people; and with its termination, and the consequent collapse of the fictitious prosperity created for certain classes, came a period of even greater pressure upon the people. From 1817 to 1848 was therefore one of almost continuous turmoil. The middle-class were striving to secure their complete control over the House of Commons by a limited extension of the suffrage, and a disfranchisement of rotten boroughs; the wage-earners were combining in all directions to obtain the suffrage for their class, but also to relieve themselves from the hideous economical injustice they suffered under. Riots in the towns and rick-burnings in the country were frequent.

The time of the fiercest struggle was shortly after the enaction of the Reform Bill of 1832. Then the effect of the New Poor Law, the constant immigration from

Ireland owing to economical causes due to landlord oppression, and the continuous operation of capitalism, produced such distress that from 1835 to 1842 the country was described by a careful foreign observer as in a state of permanent revolt. Now it was that a portion of the middle-class made common caus with the workers in their agitation; that the Trade Unionists free to combine since 1824, acted in concert to a great extent with the rank and file of labourers; and that utopian Socialism, in the shape of schemes for the nationalisation of the land, inherited from Spence and others, as well as Robert Owen's plans of co-operation, began to be recognised as a definite school.

The Trade Unionists at this time were the advanced guard of the working class party; and although, early in the day, the sense of superiority to the unskilled workers began to show itself among the members, much of the success which was obtained could never have been got without their aid. Thus the gradual enaction and enforcement of Factory Acts, in favour of the restriction of the labour of women and children within more reasonable limits as to the number of hours worked, the rights of free meeting and a free press, were obtained owing in large part to the steady organised support given by the Trade Unionists to these measures. In the chartist agitation also which was a decided movement of the proletariat against the landlord and capitalist class many Trade Unionists took an active share, as also in the serious risings which occurred in Wales, Manchester, Birmingham, Nottingham and elsewhere.

But for the counter-agitation got up by the capitalists

in favour of Free Trade in corn it is even possible that the Chartists and Socialists together might have achieved, at any rate, a temporary success for the cause of the people. As it was the Corn Law League drawing the people off on a false scent—for all can see nowadays that cheap food meant little more than increased profits for the capitalist class—the leaders were left almost without followers; and though in 1848 the renewed stir on the Continent of Europe gave the workers in this country every encouragement and an exceptional opportunity, they failed to resuscitate the energetic movement of 1842. In fact almost the only great result of all the long series of agitations for the benefit of the workers was the final settlement and consolidation in 1852 of the Factory Act of 1847.

But 1848 on the Continent of Europe was a far more important date than in England. Then first, it may be said, since Babœuf's conspiracy in 1796,—for the "Days of July" in 1830 in Paris or the outbreak at Lyons in 1834 were comparatively trifling—did the proletariat again show that it had interests which were not only not in accord with, but diametrically hostile to the interests of the middle class. All over Europe scientific, as distinguished from mere utopian, Socialism now began to be felt beneath the efforts for national independence. The famous Communist Manifesto of Marx and Engels which first formulated in a distinct shape the great truth of the inevitable struggle of classes so long as classes exist, the agitations of Blanqui and the theories of Louis Blanc, Ledru Rollin, &c., all pointed to an international combination of the workers in the interests of the labouring class which should have a far wider, nobler and more beneficial influence than endeavours, however glorious, for mere national independence. It was Socialism as an organised force based upon the sure ground of science and political economy which frightened the statesmen of all countries far more than any idea of mere national movements in which class gradations would still be maintained.

The time was not yet. The middle class triumphed not only in England but in every European country, the thousands who fell fighting for the people in Paris died vainly for the time, and the bourgeoisie gladly supported " order " under President, King, or Emperor, which ensured the butchery of the champions of the proletariat and made them certain of the continuance of the universal reign of production for profit and the consequent wage-slavery of the mass of the producers in all lands. From 1848 onwards, however, Socialism itself, international, organised Socialism, has been a moral, intellectual and physical force to be counted with in all the councils of Europe. Thenceforward the leaders of the proletariat of the world could feel assured that when the time was ripe for action they had an unshakable scientific foundation on which to build, to which indeed each year has added another layer of solid theory and fact combined.

England, unfortunately, the country where the struggle between the workers and the capitalists first took an organised and manifest shape, now, to all appearance, fell behind. The working classes of England, owing to the enormous expansion of foreign markets, to the fact that this country was the first in the field with improved machinery and highly socialised factories, to the earlier development of railways here than elsewhere, to the Free Trade Policy which kept the necessary standard of life cheap, to emigration which took off the more energetic political leaders of the people and afforded a further outlet for goods, to the stagnation of the Trade Unions which, when they had got what the higher grade of workers needed most, cared little or nothing for the welfare of the other classes of labour—the workers of England, we say, fell behind in their efforts for the enfranchisement of their class and have been content since 1848 with that moderation in their requirements and that bated breath method of urging their simplest demands which naturally find favour with their Capitalist masters.

During the thirty-five years which have passed, however, since 1848, wealth in England has increased far beyond all previous computation or imagination. From all quarters of the globe the profits of the world-market have been poured into the lap of our merchants and Capitalists. The landlords also have gained in rents, but in a very trifling degree compared with the gain of the trading class. The income tax returns alone show that the increase in assessable incomes has been from £275,000,000 in 1848 to nearly £600,000,000 in 1882. The total of realised wealth seems incredible, being given, by an official statist, at over £8,500,000,000. In every direction this expansion of wealth is to be observed. The rich quarters of our cities have spread beyond all bounds; numerous and populous lounger towns have sprung up around our coasts, where the indolent wealthy may conveniently kill time in healthy uselessness; the standard of living among the middle-class is so high that their chief diseases arise from gluttony or drink.

Yet at this very time official returns prove conclusively that vast masses of our countrymen are living on the very verge of starvation ; that much of the factory population is undergoing steady physical deterioration ; that the agricultural labourers rarely get enough food to keep them clear of diseases arising from insufficient nourishment ; while such is the housing of the wage-earners in our great cities and in our country districts that even the leading partisans of our political factions at length have awakened to the fact that civilisation for the poor has been impossible for nearly two generations under these conditions, and that some steps ought really to be taken to remedy so monstrous an evil. Drink, debauchery, vice, crime inevitably arise under such conditions. For indigestion arising from bad food, cold arising from insufficient firing, depression arising from unhealthy air and lack of amusement, necessarily drive the poor to the public-house; while even the sober have had, too often, no education which should fit them for the full enjoyment of life. And drunken and sober, virtuous and vicious—if they can be called vicious who are steeped in immorality from their very babyhood—are all subject to never-ceasing uncertainty of earning a livelihood, due to the constant introduction of fresh machines over which they have no control, or to the great commercial crises which come more frequently and last for a longer time at each recurrence. There is therefore complete anarchy of life and anarchy of production around us. Order exists, morality exists, comfort, happiness, education, as a whole, exist only for the class which has the means of production, at the expense of the class which supplies the labour-force that produces wealth.

The total income of the country is £1,300,000,000; of this the producers receive £300,000,000 in wages; and of these wages they pay back one-fifth to one-third to the landlord and capitalist class in rent, apart from the amount they refund in profits on retail and adulterated goods. The producers live on the average one-half the number of years the comfortable classes live. The total amount of property owned by 220,000 families is nearly £6,000,000,000, whilst millions are living on insufficient food and 4,500,000 persons receive charitable relief in England and Wales alone, in one shape or another, during the course of the year. The land of England is practically owned by 30,000 people against 30,000,000 and 8,000 landowners in Great Britain and Ireland receive no less than £35,000,000 a year in rents. Such plain facts as these are sufficient of themselves to show the anarchy of what we call civilisation. There have been no fewer than six commercial crises since the beginning of the century to crush the workers, not counting the Lancashire cotton famine due to the American Civil War. Meanwhile commercial war—competition in cheapness, that is, adulteration to make great profits, and attacks upon helpless people to open up new markets—has been going on all round.

Yet in the face of all this a certain school still contend that there is no class robbery; that there should be no class antagonism; that the blessings of peace and eternal money-getting for all would be ever with us if only our people—our producing people—would cease to have any families at all. What is it produces value?—labour applied to natural objects. What is it produces surplus value, and thus provides profit, interest, rent, commissions, &c.—labour applied to natural objects under the control of the capitalist class who take all the value produced less the mere average subsistence wages of the labourer. Yet to provide more wealth we are to cut off the supply of labour by breeding no labourers. This foolish Malthusian craze is itself bred of our anarchical competitive system; and those who are smitten with it cannot see that the power of man over nature is such that, if his labour were properly organised, he would produce in food or its equivalent at least four times more than the amount of wealth which he would require, if he lived in absolute comfort, provided he worked only six hours a day. Were machinery properly applied, far less than two hours labour a day for each male above twenty-one would suffice for all to live in comfort, if none lived in excessive luxury on the labour of others. As it is, about one-fourth of our adult population are engaged in actual useful production, often with inferior machinery, yet the total income is £1,300,000,000 a year.

That the power of man over nature increases in a far more rapid ratio in all progressive societies than the increase of population; that the well-to-do—such as all would be in an organised Socialist community—breed, slowly, the poor fast; that the supposed law of diminishing returns to capital (which means in one shape and another labour) expended on the soil is demonstrably false; that England alone could profitably produce food enough to feed its present population, the return increasing with each improvement in agriculture; that

North America by itself would still export enormous quantities of food after all its inhabitants were well fed even if it had 800,000,000 inhabitants: these are facts and estimates of the very highest agricultural and economical authorities which ought finally to dispose of the so-called Malthusian theory, even if the supposed necessity of fictitiously limiting the number of producers were not on the face of it an absurdity where idlers who eat enormously and produce not at all form the majority of the population.

From 1848 to 1864 there was little sign of Socialist movement of an international character, and although Lassalle's vigorous agitation in Germany which began in 1862 produced a great effect in that country no serious attempt was made to organise a general combination of Socialists until two years later. In November 1864 a meeting was held in London which laid the foundation of the International Working Men's Association. Karl Marx was the brain of the movement which soon spread to every civilised country and occasioned grave uneasiness to the courts and cabinets of Europe. The International in effect proclaimed the "Solidarity" of interest between the workers of all nations, and called upon them to unite in order to obtain control of the means of production, including the land, in every country; its leaders declared also that the war between classes in each state was the real matter of importance to the labouring class, which every where suffered from the oppression of the classes above; that therefore they should sink national differences in a great international struggle for the emancipation of the workers. These ideas obtained more ready acceptance in Germany than elsewhere as might have been expected from the superior education of the German working classes and from the fact that the heads of the movement were Germans; but up to the date of the declaration of war between France and Germany the International bid fair to become a most important body, and to combine the proletariat in a really formidable movement all over Europe.

When the war was over Paris found that though she had got rid of the Emperor with his gang of professional gamblers and prostitutes, France was to be handed to the exploitation of a reactionist Republic. The Parisians, therefore, resenting this mean substitution, made an attempt to secure perfect commercial independence before admitting the troops from without. The movement was at first necessarily in middle-class hands, and the Socialists of Paris were warned by the leaders of the International that as a simultaneous rising in Berlin, Vienna, Madrid, &c., had been impossible to arrange, failure was certain. The French Socialists were incensed at this prediction and set to work to discredit its authors. But, when the Commune had once been set on foot, it soon became clear that Paris was destined to be the scene of another bloody but again for the time, fruitless campaign of the proletariat against the bourgeoisie. Yet the champions of that class alone showed unfaltering resolution and dauntless courage in the face of danger and in the face of death.

Paris was to a large extent injured by the attacks of the troops, and partly by the action of the beaten forces of the insurgents; but the horrors of the cold-blooded massacre which followed, the infamous misdeeds of the Versailles troops, with such monsters as Gallifet at their head, and the fearful scenes on the plain of Satory have effaced almost all memory of the errors of the vanquished. Once more "order" rose in place of the best government for the many that Paris had ever seen. Throughout the world to-day the remembrance of that fearful struggle and defeat strengthens the determination of the real leaders of the proletariat revolution.

From that date forward organised Socialism has made way against many difficulties, the apathy of Englishmen having largely contributed to check any real re-commencement of the international movement. But of late years a change has taken place and the rapidly growing influence of the Democratic Federation shows that an avowed Socialist propaganda of an international character has at last taken root in this country.

What we have to face now is a bitter class antagonism between the classes who own the means of production which they use to enslave their fellows to those means of production and the labourers who are thus economically and socially enslaved. With these labourers must be numbered a large portion of the lowest middle-class who practically depend upon and are a portion of the proletariat, certain of the intellectual proletariat, clerks, &c., who are learning how they are being exploited themselves by their employers, and the domestic servants, whose servile, degraded position will be felt more and more as education spreads. Here is the last class antagonism, which indeed is world-wide—the antagonism between the slaves of the machine, the mere social engines for producing surplus value and contributing to luxury, against the capitalist class and their hangers-on, the landlords. All other antagonisms, complicated as they were, have now faded into this one simple unmistakeable hostility of clearly defined inimical interests between the proletariat and the bourgeoisie.

Proletariat production—capitalist appropriation: workers make—traders take. Socialised production; individual exchange. Work in concert: exchange at war. Supremacy of town: subservience of country. Overcrowded cities: empty fields. Such are the briefest possible statements of the economical and social forms which result in our present anarchy, not for one class alone, though that suffers far the most, but for all. And the system as a whole, is now world-wide, though in different shapes. Capital dominates the planet, acts irrespective of all nationalities, grabs its profits irrespective of all creeds and conditions: capital is international, unsectarian, destitute of regard for humanity or religion. The proletariat must learn from the system which they have to overthrow to be equally indifferent to class, creed or colour, religion or nationality, so long as the individuals sink their personal objects in a resolute endeavour against the common enemy. Unite! for this we educate, to this end we agitate, to achieve a certain victory for all we organise. Unite! Unite! Unite!

But we are all only working in a great economical movement, which we can help in some degree to advance or retard, but which will proceed whatever we do to push on or to hinder. The very conditions of production are bringing about changes in spite of the efforts of the capitalist class themselves. It has been found necessary to use the power of the State more and more to check the unbridled greed of the classes who confiscate labour. Even the middle-class debating club at Westminster, which passes muster as the English House of Commons, has found itself compelled by the exigencies of the case to interpose between the employers and their wage-slaves, between the Irish landlords and their serfs, between adulterating poisoners and their victims. The domain of laissez-faire, the hideous realm of mis-rule, has been invaded year by year by the State, controlled though it is by the oppressing classes, because some steps were absolutely essential to save the mass of the population from utter physical, moral and intellectual deterioration. Education Acts, Irish Land Acts, Employers' Liability Acts, Factory Acts, Artisans' Dwellings Acts, these and others, are direct evidence of the tendency to limit that unrestrained free contract so dear to the capitalist slave-driver of modern times. They are but half-way measures at best. What more could they be when enacted, administered and applied by the very classes which, according to the debased estimate of the aims and pleasures of life commonly held among those classes themselves, have most to lose by a thorough reorganisation? But their very appearance on the Statute Book proves that the era of middle class rule, and the period of working class apathy are alike coming to an end.

The fear of pressure from without of a threatening kind leads the luxurious classes to try to negotiate. Bankrupt of ideas, destitute of principles, their one endeavour is to compromise on favourable terms. But for us no compromise is possible which shall carry with it the continuance of the present misery.

Yet again we see the power of the State extending. It organises as well as orders, developes as well as restrains. This too in despite of huckster economy and huckster economists, whose principal professors are forced to eat their own words as administrators and to stultify their teaching as thinkers by sheer pressure of the course of events. At this hour the State is by far the largest employer of labour in the kingdom. The Post Office, the Telegraphs, the Parcels Post, the State Banks, the Arsenals, the Dockyards, the Clothing Establishments, the Army and Navy, are all managed by the State, and administered by State officials, who organise the labour below. The objection to the system is not inefficiency nor even extravagance, but the fact that those who labour are brought into competition with the lowest wages outside; and that the profits of their production or distribution are used by the State to reduce the taxation which has to be paid by the middle class.

But in this direction lies the best prospect for reform and re-organisation without bloodshed. The Railways, the Shipping Companies, the great Machine Factories, are even now ready to be handled by the State through their present officials, but under the direct control of the producing class (which will comprise the whole community) and without the endeavour to exact a profit at the expense of the overwork of the employés as is at present the case. Shareholders and factory lords have no more power, as assuredly they have no more right, than landlords to keep back that organisation of the labour of all, for the benefit of all, which is the only possible outlet from our present anarchical system of production for profit and never-ending round of commercial crises, due to the revolt of the socialised method of production against the individualised form of exchange.

When a glut of goods exists on one hand, and men eager for those goods and anxious to work stand idle and foodless on the other, when these two factors of well-being cannot be brought together *because* of the necessity to produce for profit which the very glut itself prevents, surely anarchy in production and exchange has been driven to the last ditch of absurdity. When hundreds of thousands of children are brought into the world under such conditions that good food, good health, good education, are for them impossible, the essential foundations though all three are of true morality and sound citizenship in later life, surely here too the anarchy in our commonest social relations is clearly manifested. When also we look around at the complete divison between classes, their utter ignorance of what one another think and feel, the incapacity of men and women of different classes to sit comfortably at the same meal table, though of the same race, language and creed, here, even apart from the necessary antagonism of economical interests, the social anarchy which the middle-classes call order once more stares us in the face.

After these instances of disintegration and disorder, the ugliness, waste, and adulteration seem comparatively trifling. Yet so long as competitive commerce and production for profit continue, based upon wage-slavery below, no change for the better can be wrought. As capitalism saps [all healthy social relations and reduces even the closest connection between the sexes to a mere question of bargain and sale, so it threatens to destroy the springs of all art, that is of the external beauty of life, and to reduce the world to a state of barbarism; a threat which can only be met by the demands of social order for the communising of exchange and the means of production, so that labour may be freed from the merely useless toil in which it is to a large extent at present employed, so that while machinery is used for performing labour repulsive to men, the intelligence of the workmen may be made available for the higher needs of the community, so that the greater and better part of productive labour may become a voluntary, reasonable and pleasureable exercise of the human faculties, instead of a compulsory, degrading and unhappy struggle for existence, human in nothing save its suffering, the tragedy of the battle against starvation.

How then would individuality, that unceasing cry of the bore and the dullard, be stunted by a system which should leave full play to the highest faculties of every man in return for trifling, pleasant social labour, nay, which should develope those faculties for all classes far more than they are developed to-day? Under such a system, where mankind collectively controlled their means of production, with machinery ever improving by the genius of their fellows. but used for instead of against the mass of the human race, men would at length be really free in every sense economical, social, and political, save that they would no longer possess the freedom to enslave and embrute their fellow men. Individuality is crushed to-day in every direction. The poor slave to the machine, the overworked hind or domestic drudge have no time for individuality, no strength left for their own education or development. Under our present system there is no individuality for the mass of mankind.

For re-construction and re-organisation, therefore, we Socialists continually strive, looking to the completest physical, moral and intellectual development of every human being as the highest form of the social state, as the best and truest happiness for every individual and for every class, where, as none need overwork, so none shall be able to force others to work for their profit. And this is Utopian ! Nay; it was utopian perhaps, when the powers of man over nature were trifling compared with what they are to-day, and mere division of labour almost necessarily involved the formation of castes and classes. But now steam, electricity, the forces growing daily under our hand, render equality a necessity unless barbarism and bootless destruction are to come upon us in our very midst. · For as ideas grow, as education spreads, so does the knowledge of how to turn the increasing powers of devastation to account increase among the needy and the oppressed. Gunpowder helped to sweep away feudalism with all its beauty and all its chivalry, when new forms arose from the decay of the old; now far stronger explosives are arrayed against capitalism ; while the ideas of the time are as rife with revolution as they were when feudalism fell. To avoid alike the crushing anarchy of to-day and the fierce anarchy of to-morrow, we strive to help forward the workers to the control of the State, as the only means whereby such hideous trouble can be avoided, and production and exchange can be organised for the benefit of the country at large. Thus, therefore, we propose that all should have the vote; not that the vote will free them from economical oppression, but because in this way alone is a peaceable issue possible for the possessing classes. It is better for them to yield to the vote of organised numbers than to the victory of even organised force.

What then are our objects at this hour? Some of them we have already stated. We can but point the road that we believe will be travelled in the near future. To assert definitely that this or that step must be taken at any given time would be directly contrary to our general principles, which depend for their full development upon the reasoning action of the class still to be set free. Forms of government, political devices, party arrangements, the devious tricks of faction, we contemn as useless or denounce as harmful. The only end to be sought in the organisation and representation of the people is the domination by the people of all social forces now and in the future. We claim then the land for the people, that the soil of our country with whatever is useful or beautiful in or upon it, should no longer be held by a small minority for their aggrandisement and greed, but that it should be owned by all for all collectively, to be occupied, cultivated, enjoyed, mined or built over as the majority of the people shall see fit to ordain. That the economical forms are not yet fully ready for the completest development of agricultural management is no reason why a handful of persons should draw vast revenues from a monopoly fraudulently seized from their countrymen ; still less why the land in towns, and the minerals below the land in country should be held for the benefit of the few.

But Socialists have no factious prejudices, and are influenced by no jealousies of a clique. We call therefore also for the immediate management and ownership of the railways by the State, so that the inland communications of the country may be under the control of the people at large, and carried on for their benefit, regard being had to the full remuneration of the labour of all who are engaged in the work of transport. Here is no difficulty beyond the prejudice born of a flagitious monopoly, wrongfully granted by the landlord and capitalist House of Commons in favour of the capitalist class. Labour made the railways, and living labour is confiscated daily to pay interest to the labour of the dead. It would be far better and easier for the State as the organised representative of a thorough democratic community to manage the railways through the present paid officials than to leave them under the control of a coterie of political and social adventurers, who use their railways to serve their politics, and their politics to serve their railways.

As with railways so with shipping. There the whole economical forms are ready, in the same way, for immediate management by the State, and the transfer could be arranged almost without a hitch. With mines, factories, and workshops more direct interest by the workers engaged in them would be needed, but as education extends, and the habit of economical collective freedom grows, it will be as easy for the labourers to choose their own superintendents, and apply the best machinery, as it is for the capitalist to choose and use them to-day. The inventor, the organiser, the manager are not the people who sweep off the bulk of the surplus value made by labour as it is, but the idle, useless capitalists who sit at home and appropriate other men's work by means of social conventions which they themselves have formulated, and they themselves give effect to by force of law.

Similarly the handling of money and credit must necessarily be carried on in future for the advantage of the community at large. National banks, national credit establishments, State and Communal centres of distribution for the purchase and exchange of goods will supplant and take over the huge enterprises for the gain of a class which now exercise such enormous influence, and accumulate such vast profits under protection of the middle-class State. As production is inevitably social, exchange must be social too. Simply as a stepping-stone to the attainment of this State organisation of production and exchange do we advocate the heaviest cumulative taxation rising upon all incomes derived from trade or business, as well as upon those drawn from the land. Only by collective superintendence of production and exchange, only by the scientific organisation of labour at home and supply of markets abroad, can our present anarchy be put an end to, and a better system be allowed to grow up. Removal and reconstruction must go on together, and at the same time. The very existence and increase of Companies, the very development of State management now going on, point out clearly the lines of necessary progress: with the complete organisation of democracy the State, in its present meaning of class predominance, necessarily disappears.

But this is confiscation. Far from it, it is restitution. Those who cry for compensation for past robbery, and shriek confiscation because the right to rob in future is challenged, should bear in mind that the men and women whom we would compensate are those who are now stumbling half-clothed and half-fed from a pauper cradle to a pauper grave, in order that capitalists and landlords may live in luxury and excess. The dead have passed beyond compensation: it will be well if the living do not call for vengeance on their behalf. Our first principle as Socialists is that all should be well-fed, well-housed, well-educated. For this object we urge forward the Revolution which our enemies hysterically shriek at, and frantically try to dam back. But we mean wrong to none. Rather would we claim the aid of such of the luxurious classes as are willing, so long as they have still enough and to spare, to forego the frightful privilege of feeding fat upon the wretchedness of others. Good housing for all cannot be got if greed is to organise the new arrangements: good food and physical, mental, and moral education for all classes cannot be obtained if factitious superiority and harmful social distinctions are to be kept up.

Therefore, we say once more this *is* a class war; we know it; we are preparing for it; we rejoice at its near approach. We mean to break down competition, and to substitute universal organisation and co-operation. There lie around us the necessary methods: they need but to be applied. But there are many difficulties and dangers, the power of wealth is great, the unscrupulousness of property knows no bounds ? We are well aware of this : we see and do not shrink from the inevitable struggle. But the numbers over against us, the hosts who may be bribed to fight for their oppressors, even to their own hurt ; there are thousands, perhaps millions, of such men ? There are. We know that too. But in a cause like ours, we refuse to recognise difficulties, with such misery around us we cannot stop to calculate forces, with such a future before us we will never count heads.

The Revolution is prepared in the womb of society, it needs but one strenous and organised effort to manifest the new period in legal and acknowledged shape to the world. To attempt to return to the old forms of individual production, would be at the same reactionary and anarchical. We cannot, if we would, so put back the hands upon the dial of human development. It is nowise desirable we should. The increased power of man over nature is gained by co-operation, by social machinery, by associated labour, by skilfully concerted work. This has been due to countless ages of growth and development, involving often the most horrible oppression, but ever producing more wealth with less labour. We inherit the results of this long martyrdom of man to the forms of production and exchange. It is for us to take hold of and use these improvements for the enfranchisement of the people, and for the establishment of happiness and organised contentment for mankind. We in England have arrived at the completest economical development. Our example therefore, will guide and encourage the world. All over the planet the same ideas are abroad. In Germany, France, Scandinavia, Russia, Italy, Spain, far away in the ancient empires of Asia, as well as in America, and the other flourishing Colonies of our days, the labourers stretch out their hands to one another for help, co-operation and encouragement in the struggle which manifestly draws near. Confident in their cause the Socialists alone of modern parties can march steadily forward in international comity, to the assurance of victory for all.

Thus then, based upon science and political economy, rejoicing in the beauty of an enfranchised art, with our social creed as our only religion—the scientific organisation of labour, and the universal brotherhood of man—we appeal to men and women of all classes, all creeds and all nationalities to join us in the struggle wherein none can fail, to prepare for themselves, and for their children a nobler, higher lot than has hitherto been theirs, and to pass on to countless generations that joy, that beauty and that perfect contentment which can arise from true Socialism alone.

Signed the EXECUTIVE COMMITTEE OF THE DEMOCRATIC FEDERATION,

E. BELFORT BAX.	J. L. JOYNES.
HERBERT BURROWS.	TOM. S. LEMON.
R. D. BUTLER.	JAMES MACDONALD.
H. H. CHAMPION, *Hon. Secretary.*	WILLIAM MORRIS, *Hon. Treasurer*
W. J. CLARK, *Lecture Secretary.*	JAMES F. MURRAY.
	H. QUELCH.
H. A. FULLER.	A. SCHEU.
H. M. HYNDMAN, *Chairman.*	HELEN TAYLOR.
	JOHN E. WILLIAMS.

THE MODERN PRESS.

16 pp., Crown 8vo, in wrapper.

SOCIALISM *versus* SMITHISM,

An open letter from H. M. HYNDMAN to SAMUEL SMITH, M.P. for Liverpool.

PRICE ONE PENNY.

** A reply to an attack by Mr. Smith on "Socialism made Plain," the manifesto issued by the Democratic Federation.

PRICE SIXPENCE. (*Cloth* 1/6)

NEW BOOK OF KINGS,

BY. J. MORRISON DAVIDSON.
(Of the Middle Temple)
Barrister-at Law.

Henry George says:—" It would be a great thing if it could be scattered broadcast over England by hundreds of thousands."
"Vivacious and trenchant. . . . Is calculated to open the eyes of people who now worship monarchy as a fetish."—*London Echo*.

PRICE SIXPENCE. *Cloth*, 1/6

THE BOOK OF LORDS,

A SEQUEL TO THE NEW BOOK OF KINGS.

BY

J. MORRISON DAVIDSON.
(Of the Middle Temple)
Barrister-at Law.

SEVENTH EDITION.

THE ADVENTURES OF A TOURIST IN IRELAND.

BY. J. L. JOYNES.

Second Edition, (Reduced to) 1s.

SOCIALISM AND SLAVERY,

A reply to Mr. HERBERT SPENCER's Article on "THE COMING SLAVERY," by H. M. HYNDMAN. PRICE 1d.

THE MODERN PRESS.

NOW READY, PRICE SIXPENCE.

The Working Man's Programme,

(ARBEITER-PROGRAMM.)

By FERDINAND LASSALLE.

Translated by EDWARD PETERS *(late of the Madras Civil Service).*

Cr. 8vo., SIXPENCE.

COMING REVOLUTION IN ENGLAND.

By H. M. HYNDMAN.

Cr. 8vo., SIXPENCE.

SOCIAL RECONSTRUCTION OF ENGLAND.

By H. M. HYNDMAN.

Demy 8vo., in wrapper, SIXPENCE.

THE

ROBBERY OF THE POOR.

By W. H. P. CAMPBELL.

The writer shows in this pamphlet the justice of the attack of the Socialists on private property and vindicates the right to "expropriate the expropriators."